MAN
MADE

Chris De Man
Don Pearson
Ben Arendt

pot-boilers

Requests for permission should be made in writing to:
Pot-Boilers, 100 Stevens St. SW, Grand Rapids, MI 49507

www.pot-boilers.com

Book jacket design & layout by Deksia Design LLC.

ISBN 13 / 978-0-578-10319-8

Manufactured in the United States of America
1 2 3 56 78 23 23 11

To our dads who made us men,
our wives who make us better and our kids
who keep us humble.

Contents

Introduction

Thom watched his five-year-old son attempt to untangle himself from the bike wreckage amidst a flood of tears and frustration. *Should've left the training wheels on*, he muttered to himself as he hurried to the crash site. *This one isn't going to be pretty.*

Becoming a man isn't pretty either. Boys don't simply become men. There is no manual. You can't just add water. And it can't be delegated to…her.

Boys are man-made.

But in one of history's most bizarre reversals, western culture has recently given up on rites of passage—those man-made experiences where young males are initiated into the brotherhood of men. It's inconceivable that after thousands of years of human experience we've abandoned this process.

Previous generations were more intentional with boy raising. Men took an approach that was somewhat ruthless. Some might call it calloused, even heartless as men placed their boys in situations where they had to face their fears—and death. When confronted with well-constructed challenges, boys grow into men. They find something deep within themselves they didn't know existed. Such discovery is crucial to the development of manly character.

Making men from boys has always been part of life's progression, but culture's recent dismantling of men has created a crisis. A man crisis.

So what's to be done? We could play it safe. Ignore the crisis. Let our boys drift on the sea of culture hoping they find their way to 'man land.' Or we can get about the noble task of making boys into men. Accept responsibility for our God-given role and show young men the path to authentic, God-honoring, manly living.

That path moves through stages. Each stage revolves around core issues fathers and father figures must bring to life for their boys. Through purposeful and natural growing-up experiences, such issues are developed and processed as a boy is transported toward manhood.

Helping make men from boys is what this short book is about. Through stories we'll help you identify the 'Big Idea' at each stage of the game. We'll also suggest experiences for your 'Manhood Backpack' aimed at creating a customized journey into manhood for your son.

The process doesn't just happen. It's man-made. And you're the man.

Stage 01 Awaken

(Ages 5-10)

"The desire for safety stands against every great and noble enterprise."

– Cornelius Tacitus, 1st Century A.D. Roman Historian and Politician

---

"The only man who never makes a mistake is the man who never does anything."

– Teddy Roosevelt

Ben Arendt

The Rungu

A few months ago when I was in rural Kenya, I spent time in remote villages visiting Massai tribes. The Massai are resourceful people with a society steeped in tradition. Their traditions impact everything from bright colors on clothing to farming.

During my first visit, I was greeted outside the community gate by two young men in crimson red robes, beaded necklaces and ornamental earrings. I quickly noticed that on their belts they carried wooden weapons. These men were elders sent by the chief to meet me before I was allowed to enter. I didn't know what to do, and certainly didn't know what to say. How do I strike up a conversation? It's not like I can start with, "So do you guys really think Lee Harvey Oswald acted alone?"

Only one thing came to mind. Trying to break the ice, I nervously asked if I could take a photograph with them. As I asked, the men turned quickly, whistled and signaled to a young boy. I made eye contact with the boy and tried to cross-culturally plead with him to not get the secret marinade they would use as they slow cooked me over an open fire.

The boy disappeared.

Ever seen the commercials that end with, "Want to get away?"

A few moments later the boy came running towards us with a gleeful smile. In his hands he was carrying what looked like a large ball of fur. Without acknowledging the boy or saying a word to me, the men took the fur ball and placed it on my head.

What I was wearing was a headdress made solely from a lion's mane. And as I wore it, something special happened. I could feel that headdress throughout my entire body. And what I felt wasn't the fur. It was honor.

Now we were ready for the photograph.

Later, my new friends described to me the unique symbolism of the headdress. It represents a boy's rite of passage into manhood. The Massai are intentional with making men from their boys. Around age 13, young Massai males are swept into an experience that has been passed through the generations. Using only a wooden club (exactly the same as the ones on the elder's belts) called a rungu, the boys are tasked with finding, stalking and killing a lion. Once the feat of lion killing is accomplished, the lion and boy are brought back to the village. There, the elders and chief gather the tribe. In the midst of this community, a cow is brought forward as the ceremony begins. A small incision is made in the cow's neck and blood is collected in a bowl. Then, in plain view for all to see, the rungu wielding, lion-killing boy drinks the blood and is ceremonially transformed into a warrior. He is now a man.

As I write this I can't help but think of that young boy who watched me enter his village. With just a simple, unspoken motion he ran to get the mane. As he did, it was if something in him anticipated his moment. The moment when he would wear the headdress and become part of the community of men.

So, how do boys become men?

What events, activities or experiences help transition boys into manhood?

Are these moments only symbolic?

Is tradition enough?

What part does the community of men play?

Must there be elements of risk and adventure?

I ask these questions because after my encounter in that village I couldn't help but wonder: What rites of passage will my son experience? I have to admit that initially I couldn't think of what would qualify as a rite of passage. Not just for him, but for his friends, for my community.

The fact is our boys do go through rites of passage. But many of them go undetected. Unlike the Massai, much of what we think makes men from boys does not include risk, pain or community. Instead of facing a lion with a rungu, our boys might perceive manliness through acquiring things or feeling accepted. Obtaining things like their first cell phone, buying and wearing expensive (or the right) pair of jeans, purchasing the newest game console or getting the keys to the car. This path to manhood by acquisition stands in contrast to a community of men celebrating and welcoming a boy into manhood through trial and perseverance.

After spending a month in Kenya, I left inspired to provide clear, recognizable, and anticipated rites of passage for my boy. And, I couldn't come home without gifts for my children. As you can probably guess, the gift I brought home for my son was a rungu. As I laid the weapon in my son's eager hands, I told him about the celebrated club of East Africa. I described the brave men I'd met. I explained their solidarity. I told him about the killing of lions, the cow's blood and the ceremony. I talked about the lion's mane headdress.

That gift set the stage for me to cast a vision. It gave us an opportunity together. A chance for me to communicate to him that I want to see him become a warrior who takes risks, is courageous and deals with the unavoidable pain of life. It was a great father-son moment. But the day-to-day challenge now is to encourage my boy, who is less than ten, to be that warrior—especially when I don't feel like one myself.

T.S. Elliot once wrote, "We had the experience but we missed the meaning." My Kenyan experience was a gift. But if I leave that experience wrapped in the gift of a souvenir wooden club, I've missed the point. The experience is meaningful when the significance of the rungu is translated into words that speak life into my son.

Experiences can be small. They can be big. They can be complex. They can be simple. It's okay if they look different for you than they do for me. Yet, the business of man-making starts now. And it requires me, as his father, to engage all aspects of his life—including those things that may feel awkward, remind me of my past, or bring me to shame. It requires me to not just create experiences, but provide meaning and direction.

I want to make an impact on my son. The fact is, I will make an impact.

So will you.

Man-Cation

A friend of mine told me a story about the awkwardness associated with learning about sex. As a young man approaching adolescence, he remembers his mother having 'the talk' with him. His mother went to great lengths explaining the differences between boys and girls, the changes he would soon experience in his body, and a yet to come attraction for the opposite sex. She also told him where babies come from. After she finished the lesson, in a moment of innocence he asked, "So, does dad know any of this?"

Funny story, yes. But it's also sad. It's not sad because of his mother's presence but because of his father's absence. Fathers need to enter their son's story with clarity and strength. That doesn't mean we have to have all the answers. I am definitely clumsy. Rarely do I know with absolute certainty what to do or how to pursue my boy. But I must. It's my job to authenticate manhood to my son.

An important goal for this Awaken stage is for me to be the one man in my son's life that he can count on. I need to be trusted to give my best, work hard, be faithful, show affection and be vulnerable. I started to really get traction with these things the summer my son was five years old.

That summer I told him that we were going on our first ever 'man-cation.' Just the two of us for a long weekend in the woods. We've done it every summer since and it has become the most anticipated tradition we have.

Our man-cations have taken us to remote islands in the middle of Lake Michigan. We've camped by streams and hiked mountains in Colorado. Man-cation basics include making dinners over a fire, challenging physical activity and intentional, age-appropriate conversation. I go into the weekend with a game plan. I have themes in mind. Topics to cover.

I remember a conversation during one of our man-cations when my son was eight. I had decided it was time to be direct with our first conversation about sex. We had just finished our annual spaghetti meal and were sitting together around the fire. The sun was setting over Lake Michigan, which provided a great metaphor for the awkward subject matter. I had felt pressure for years about this moment and it was finally here. How many of your friends mock 'the talk' they had with their fathers (or mothers in some cases)? I was worried I would get it wrong.

I got things started by speaking about the beauty of the water. It's resourcefulness and how it fosters life. How it's a resource we need to care for. We also talked about fire. We discussed how the fire was keeping us warm, and how it helped us create a delicious meal.

Water and fire. Good things. Helpful things. But there was more. I asked my son how water and fire might cause damage – to a forest, a city, a person. It became obvious that water and fire can heal or harm. Once that connection was made, we were ready (I thought) to talk about sex.

I didn't really know what to do or say. But I knew I had to say something. So I went for it. I asked my boy how he thought a baby enters the world. I listened to his hypothesis and then simply told him how reproduction occurs, with age appropriate details. I told him that sex is a beautiful thing that God intended for a husband and wife to experience in marriage. Sex is something that gives and creates life. It's an expression of the deepest parts of who we are in the special relationship of covenant marriage.

About two weeks after this first sex talk, I asked my son, "Where does a baby come from?" He did pretty well with the necessary details. I continue to check in with him every couple of months. Using simple things like water and fire I was able to introduce, on a basic level, something complex like sexuality which is both wonderful, and at times destructive. Sure, some of the big concepts he might not get at this stage. But eventually he will. I want to work hard to create openness in our relationship. I don't want to get bogged-down in awkward feelings, shame, pressure and confusion.

The choices we make sexually have life-long implications. As men, we must be diligent and wise in the training of our boys. We must encourage dialogue and be a safe sounding board. Sexual tension only grows as a boy progress through the stages of manhood. So start talking sex—now!

Pencil & Paper

Almost a year ago my wife (the most gifted woman I know) and I were hiking some trails along a river near our house. As we walked she expressed concern over my son's writing and spelling abilities. She explained he was easily frustrated by the spelling errors he would make on school assignments. When asked to express himself with words, he would get emotional, tense up and shut down. He found it difficult to write out a simple page of thoughts. As we walked the trail that day, she expressed that she was out of motivational ideas.

I am not sure how, but something came to mind. Really, I have like one good idea every leap year. I asked her if it would be okay if I started a journal with him. She assured me it would never work, but she was open to anything. That night I went to my son and asked him if I could write him questions and thoughts in a notebook. I asked if he would do the same for me. I told him no topics were off limits, he could write as little or as much as he wanted, and he could take his time to get back to me. To my (and my wife's) surprise, he excitedly agreed.

My entries include encouragement, something I've noticed about him or something I want him to know. Sometimes I just try to be funny. Other times I ask him to be reflective. Many times I will do a series of fill-in-the-blanks. Often times I use it as an opportunity to seek his advice. Here are a few excerpts:

"...wow you are getting good at shooting hoops. I love spending time with you doing just about anything, but there is something about basketball in the driveway... I love it. How are you feeling in general about your skills? Would you say you are feeling confident? Anything you are afraid of right now?"

"So today was a tough one. There is a guy I know that I am really struggling with. To be honest I have a bad attitude and I need help. Here's the situation and I need your advice: this person tends to be negative and critical (kind of like me) and we don't see eye to eye. I have talked about him behind his back and not to his face. And when I do, I am not saying nice things about him. HELP!"

Fill In The Blank

I am so excited about ———————————————————

Sometimes I wonder why God————————————————

I have been fearful that ————————————————————

I am working on _____

My favorite thing to do is _____

Top 10 summer highlights are _____

The responses have been amazing. This written exchange has opened a window into my son's soul that I otherwise would never see. He is honest, forthright and funny. It's touching. Through this simple notebook and pencil, I want to teach him humility. I want him to know I make mistakes. I want to ask him for advice, not just give it. I want to expand my wonder of who he is and what he thinks. I want to ask, and be asked embarrassing questions. Our written exchange is one way to form a trusting relationship that better handles the disappointments, mistakes and joys that will come – with accelerating speed – in the years ahead.

Work

I hate winter. My mom told me to never use that word. But seriously, I hate winter. It's cold. It's grey. It's windy. Where I live winter holds the calendar hostage for over nine months. The sun rises around noon and then sets at 3 p.m. Okay, I am being dramatic, but I am trying to make a point: I hate winter.

When my son was two-and-a-half years old he received his first snow shovel. During that winter, I recall a pretty nasty snowfall that left eight inches overnight. The following morning I forced myself to get up early to work on my attitude—and the driveway.

My son awoke that morning to sounds of my shovel scraping the driveway outside his window. He went straight to his mom, woke her up and asked if he could go outside and join me. She agreed, bundled him up in his oversized coat and mittens and opened the door. I remember seeing her standing in the open doorway on the porch with my eager son smiling at me. I looked at my wife, paused, and while glancing down at my knee-high son I asked out loud, "What's he going to do out here?"

Talk about missing the meaning!

My wife, who should have hit me with a snowball, asked me to get his mini shovel out of the garage. I reluctantly agreed. It wasn't that I didn't want my son to be around. What I wanted was to get the work done, and I knew he would slow me down.

It took me nearly two hours to clear the driveway that morning. My son was with me the entire time. I could not believe it. Not once did he ask to go back inside the house. Not once did he cry because he was cold. Not once did he actually get one shovel scoop of snow off the driveway. For the entire winter he was my snow-shoveling shadow. Early mornings or freezing cold, it didn't matter. He was there—with me.

As winter wore on, I began to anticipate snow fall. In fact, I actually wanted it to snow. My son and I would clear the driveway, stand back and look at what we accomplished. Together. To this day, he still asks me to wake him up when it snows.

I have had numerous projects throughout the years that have taken me three times longer to complete because I have allowed, asked and wanted my son to join in on the work. I want him to see that work is challenging yet deeply satisfying. As I engage my son in these working experiences, there's a shared satisfaction as his sense of responsibility builds and I help ignite his desire for manly living.

Wrap-Up

For you it might not be a trip to Africa to get a rungu. Maybe you'll never set sail on a "man-cation." Perhaps writing isn't your thing. Maybe you have a snow blower because your brain actually works. Whatever your gifts are and however your son is wired, work towards meaningful experiences. Listen to music together. Play catch. Create art. Talk. Fish. Wrestle. Study cars. Work on the lawn. Whatever makes a connection, do it together. It's less about the experience and more about the meaning. What does the experience lead to? It will lead to nowhere if you don't have direction behind the experiences you craft for your son.

Manhood Backpack / Awaken Stage

Big Idea / Invite your son into the everyday of manly living.
Call to Action / Craft meaningful experiences for you and your son.

Options for Action

01 / Man-cation
02 / Build something together
03 / Disassemble something together (engine, old electronics) and recycle for cash
04 / Journal together
05 / Go for extended bike rides
06 / Get a GPS and go Geo Caching
07 / Attend Civil War Reenactments
08 / Teach him to play chess (or learn together)
09 / Coach one of his teams—athletic or otherwise
10 / Start a collection together
11 / Do a social service project together (soup kitchen)
12 / Have him keep something alive that isn't a pet (a plant, garden, chickens for eggs, cow)

Time Out

"But God is faithful and fair. If we admit that we have sinned, he will forgive us our sins. He will forgive every wrong thing we have done. He will make us pure."

The Bible | 1 John 1:9 (NIRV)

"God is always covering our nakedness and silencing our shame."

– **Richard Rohr**

Disqualified?

One barrier to being open with our boys about sexuality is our own shame. Shame from the load of sexual baggage many of us carry—past and present. Porn. Partners. Lustful masturbation. Same-sex attraction. It's easy to think our own sexual rap-sheet disqualifies us from speaking authoritatively to our sons. We feel like hypocrites. How can we speak to our boys about sex when we've fumbled the ball so many times?

Well, we can. Why? Because each of us fail in some way. But it is in those failures we experience grace—grace that qualifies us to speak. In fact, through God's abundant grace we are overqualified. Plus, it's our responsibility to talk with our boys—so we must. It's risky, for sure. But bringing a boy into manhood means going to the edge of what's comfortable—and then taking another step.

We can't sit idle. We live in a pornographic culture. Sex sells. Marketing is erotic and all media is sensual. The checkout line at the grocery store is an assault. I have to be my son's protector. To avoid talking about the cultural assault is easy. But being a man means I engage and explain. It means I own the responsibility to be frank with my son about sexual feelings and impulses. To talk about the desires God has given us. To teach him to battle for God's design for sex which means restraint, control, a purified mind and endurance. Waiting around until my son has a problem or starts asking questions is unacceptable. As a dad, I must prepare for what's ahead. I need a strategy for uncomfortable topics like masturbation, physical contact with girls and pornography.

So I'm present with my son in his struggle. I start by admitting my struggle. On a regular basis I tell my son, "I am a struggler;

you are a struggler; you live in a family of strugglers." We can't eliminate struggle, so we enter it. I urge my boy to struggle well. I set high standards—for me, and my son. I encourage conversation. I want to know what he is thinking, feeling, hearing and observing. In return, I'm honest with him. I want my son to hear from me, "I've been there. In many ways, I am there." We meet the struggle of male sexuality—together.

All men need the support and involvement of other men. We need communities where fathers are talking honestly with their sons about sex. Let's bring these conversations to the living room instead of relying on perverted playground dialogue.

This is big stuff. Don't fight alone. Don't hide behind your past. You are qualified to protect and prepare your boy. So be that man—because you are.

Shhh...It's a Secret

Still, you might be thinking, "I agree about the protect and prepare stuff. And yes, I do what to give my son good perspective on sexuality. The problem is I've got junk. My life is still a mess. I don't think I'm the right guy to speak to my son about things manly—sex or otherwise. No one really knows what's going on for me. I've kept things tight. And I'd like to keep it that way."

Secrets. We've all got them. A while back my son told me one of his. It was a secret held close for quite some time. It wasn't the fun, surprise party kind of secret. It was big. Burdening. Volatile. It was festering in a cloak of darkness. A secret that had secrets of its own, which it whispered into my son's self talk. Lies, actually. Words from the pit. Poisonous arguments meant to bind my son in silence. A silence that fed the secret and kept it safe.

But here's a truth about secrets: a secret revealed has no power. That's great encouragement, especially for those secrets we want hidden forever. Secrets that we fear, once known, will make us unlovable. I saw that fear in my son as he voiced his secret with a nervous courage. But as he found expression for his secret, wonderful moments of victory erupted. A door tightly closed burst open. In the telling of what was hidden, my son was freed from a silent prison. A prison of darkness, deception and guilt. Physical and emotional expressions of relief ensued. We celebrated as the power drained from a secret held painfully tight for too long.

John Piper said, "God often disapproves of his children's behavior. But he never treats us with contempt." I have to admit that too often my son has felt my disapproval. Historically, my relating with him has tilted toward contempt—sometimes subtle, other times overt and judgmental. When really upset, I've been known to launch into a rehash of a tired 3-point sermon. Those are not my best moments. And that's not how I would want to be treated. Nor it is how God treats me.

Making a man of your son will cause you to evaluate your own journey toward manhood. It will challenge you in your failures. It will expose your secret struggles. It will refresh hurts from the past. And for some, it will accent the absence of your father's participation in your becoming a man.

Yet despite our junk, there is hope. Jesus offers us grace for all our nastiness. He receives us, not because of what we do, but because of who He is (Titus 3:5). He can handle our disappointment, regret and fear. He can heal past hurts and give strength for struggles in the present.

Forgiveness is a great place to start. Talk to God about the past and present. Ask Him for wisdom to use your experiences in ways that make you a better father. Forgive yourself. Your father. Others in your past that have hurt you physically or emotionally. Bury grudges. Let go of regret. Expose your secrets. Confess and reconcile.

We look back, so we can move forward. Leverage the good, the bad and the ugly of your story to equip your son to be a man of integrity. Secrets and otherwise, you're the best man to pace with your son along the road to manhood.

Stage 02 Activate

(Ages 10-13)

"That's what fathering is all about. It's mentoring and equipping your son to become a man who will assume the family leadership for the next generation. You have no higher calling in life. It is your God-given assignment."

– Steve Farrar

"The character of life isn't set in ten big moments. The character of life is set in 10,000 little moments of everyday life."

– Paul David Tripp

Chris De Man

Mini-me

I have spies in my house. They watch, listen, observe, mimic. If you're a dad, you've got spies too.

Boys and young men constantly watch and glean bits of manliness from grown men. Even the smallest details get etched into boyhood memories. Much of what a boy learns about manly living is caught.

In my growing-up years, I spent hours observing my dad. I would watch him go about the work of running our home. From fixing all that was broken to mowing the lawn to building a shed. I was his shadow—sometimes seen, sometimes not. And sometimes too close.

I memorized dad's mannerisms, his expressions, his patterns, his methods. I learned his classic phrases like "measure twice, cut once", "never do half a job", and the well-known "lefty-loosey, righty-tighty." I remember him smelling of hard work—sweat, dirt, fuel and paint. I wondered at his rock-steady hand that could cut-in paint along any ceiling like Michelangelo. I marveled at his ability to coax the rusted bolt loose. Sometime he went shirtless. Often got sunburned. There were cuts and scrapes, but he continued unfazed.

And then there were dad's muscles. There wasn't a pickle jar dad couldn't open. Even the most stubborn jar relinquished its seal to dad with a 'pop.' Whether busting through pickle jars or hanging drywall, I was fascinated with dad's strength. I frequently stole glances at the muscle in the crook of his lower and upper arm. It bulged when he gripped, lifted or just wrote with a pencil. He was tough. His muscle was cool. I wanted one.

I remember wondering if my forearm would someday look like

his. I would bend my arm and flex, looking with hope for the desired mound of muscle. Bend, flex, look, repeat.

I'm still looking.

Dad often closed a hard day's work by grabbing a beat-up, translucent white, two-quart pitcher. He'd fill it half water, half ice. Then he'd stand – not sit – and relieve a bit of his exhaustion with large gulps. He looked like Mean Joe Greene downing a bottle of Coca-Cola. As I took-in those moments, I pondered how manly it was to drink straight from a pitcher. To tame two quarts of ice water in a few short minutes. To feel the satisfaction of a hard day's work. To be master of a small suburban homestead.

Because manliness is stamped upon my soul, something deep inside me stirred to life as I watched my dad work. As I admired his strength. As I pondered his painting prowess. Even in his drinking he was, at least in my eyes, the epitome of manliness. And I wanted to be just like him.

Questions

It's natural and right for boys to look to their fathers for manly cues. To copy their actions. To assimilate their attitudes and perspectives. The challenge for us as men is to give them something worth imitating.

Like I looked to my dad for manly behavior, so my sons now look to me. They may not be looking at my forearms, but they watch closely for whatever they think defines authentic manhood. And as they look they are thinking about themselves. They are pondering, comparing, wondering and questioning. They're envisioning a future when they will be build a shed, paint their home and bust loose rusty bolts. In this Activate stage, your boy is beginning to wrestle with whether he has manly potential. An internal turmoil starts brewing as he asks two primary questions: "What does it take to be a man?" and "Have I got it?"

All men must answer those questions. They exist at the core of what defines a man. They bully our struggle of passivity and inadequacy. And in good and bad ways, all men do find answers. Some through power. Others choose money. And there's always the allure of sexual adventure. Out of balance, those things lead to empty, boyish living. As fathers, we have a great responsibility (and privilege) to help our sons with biblical answers to their deepest questions.

Another question men desperately need answered is this: "When do I become a man?" Seems like a ridiculous question, but it's not. Unlike women who have a built-in, monthly reminder of their womanhood, young men are left to wonder when they've walked through the gate into man land. Many adult men live with a boy complex. Sure, they may have full-grown bodies, but they feel small. Inadequate. Incapable. Like a boy. Why?

For many guys it's because they can't go back to a definitive time, place or experience when they formally left boy-world and entered the community of men. Yes, all boys grow into adult males. But age, body hair and the ability to procreate are not the only qualifiers of manhood. Nor are forearm muscles or the ability to quaff a pitcher of ice water. Manhood is learned and earned. It's observed, mimicked and reproduced. It's authenticated in young men by grown men who have answered the questions of manhood themselves. Men who are far from perfect, but have summoned the courage to push beyond their fears.

You can be that man. You must be that man. For you, and your boy. Help your son get his questions about manhood answered. Let's not be responsible for raising a generation of adult-bodied men who think, act and speak like boys.

Many of us know men who haven't progressed beyond a prepubescent maturity. It's tragic. In his Men's Fraternity curriculum, Robert Lewis gives this stark command to grown men: "The boy in you must die!" Such death is required so manliness can flourish. Boys need men. Girls need men. Women need men—men of humble courage who give, serve, lead and love.

So what do we do? How do we authenticate manhood? How does a man gently but intentionally move his boy through the death of boyhood and on to manliness?

Man Wall

One way I've been intentional with the dying process is by creating a Man Wall. Just outside the bedroom my three boys call home is a small section of hallway. It's a six foot stretch in which no Barbies, butterflies, American Girl Dolls or stuffed unicorns are permitted. My boys and I painted the walls shades of tan and brown. We outfitted (not decorated) the wall with rough and untamed things like weather-worn boards and rusty nails. It's not extravagant, but it is a hallowed, manly space.

Also on our Man Wall hang swords. Serious swords. Heavy, dangerous, lethal swords. Swords that signify something special for me and my tribe of men-in-training. Presently, two swords hang in place—mine, and that of my oldest son. Above each sword is a simple placard bearing our name. Next to our swords are two more placards that sit atop sword hangers—which are empty. Empty because the swords that will occupy those hangers have yet to be conferred upon my younger sons.

In my home, swords are given at age 13. They're delivered with celebration and ceremony in the context of community. I gather trusted, godly men to praise, encourage and challenge my son. These men write and read letters. Prayers are spoken. Hands are laid. It's a rite of passage. A definitive moment when the boy starts to die and the man starts to live.

Our Man Wall is a North Star of sorts, pointing my boys toward the manly life for which they were created. Every time my boys walk down that hallway, they are confronted with their destiny.

Not long ago I was having a conversation with one of my sons. It started with a simple question that quickly took us into some pretty thick issues. The discussion turned serious. It was necessary, but painful. A few minutes into the conversation, my son began reflecting on our Man Wall. Those reflections brought tears. Tears of sadness. My son was feeling unworthy of what the Man Wall represented. He was burdened with the lie that he doesn't have what it takes to be a real man. He considered himself disqualified from placing his sword on the wall next to the others.

This moment of reflection was particularly heavy for my boy because he was less than a year away from filling his empty sword hanger. Receiving, holding and hanging that sword is a big deal for my clan. It should be. Being a biblically authentic man is a noble task.

As a father, this conversation brought sorrow and excitement. Sorrow because of the pain and disgrace my son felt. But excitement for the tension the Man Wall was creating. I was encouraged by my boy's desire to be a genuine man. He was craving manhood. He was asking, "Do I have what it takes?" Even better, he was asking it with me, his dad. His greatest influence. The one he is likely watching very closely. Copying. Admiring.

Curiosities

Moving a boy along the path to manliness requires much more than swords. As boys enter the pre-teen years, curiosities go beyond why the sky is blue. Dreams of wanting to be a fireman or superhero are replaced with musings about self worth, physical stature, and maybe even…girls. Eventually, a boy's mind fosters curiosities about sex.

It's ironic that a subject so hand-in-glove with masculinity creates great embarrassment and secrecy. Some men cower and bust a cold sweat when it comes to talking sex with their children. Yet, God's instruction for men to work and protect (The Bible, Genesis 2:15) certainly applies to sexual behavior. The stewardship of sexuality is not caught, but taught. Unfortunately, we don't lack for 'teachers.' The problem is those teachers deliver instruction counter to God's intent.

Our culture depicts men as animals. Puppy dogs panting for sexual treats. Insatiable. Predictable. Incompetent couch dwellers living only for the next sporting event, pizza delivery and sexual opportunity—real or virtual. Women tease. Men gawk. It's a sad twisting of roles and despicable stereotyping. Unfortunately, there's ample reason within the community of men to support such perceptions.

So where does a boy develop his story about sex? Left to wander through culture on his own, he'll get it through viewing thousands of advertisements, rescuing busty video game babes and feasting on a diet of innuendo and double-entendre. His world is infiltrated with pornographic material.

He'll be stimulated then desensitized by women who dress too tight with too little. Aggressive females will prey on his lusts. He'll be told same-sex attraction is a human rights issue. That self stimulation is normal, expected and a legitimate way to manage sexual tension.

What's the antidote for our sex-drunk culture? A godly father. A man who will tell the truth about a man's sexuality. Straight talk in age-appropriate ways. Every boy needs a father or mentor who understands sex has nothing to do with birds or bees. That sexuality goes beyond biology. Peer pressure, drive, curiosities, feelings, manipulation and masturbation are part of the sex package that needs opportunity to be taught and discussed.

I've already said it: talking sex isn't easy. Sex is a wonderfully weird concept. That's why talking about it can seem worse than a root canal. Your boy feels the same way. During talks with my sons, I've found their interest is more about the donut I've bribed them with than my well-rehearsed presentation (complete with diagrams) of the reproductive process. But don't let their sugar-coated face fool you. They're listening. Want proof? I can almost guarantee that within a few weeks your boy will be back with questions.

Like when you're working in the garage. Your son will meander over and pop a question about erections (pun intended). That's just how it works. But it's good. Better that he ask you than his buddy. Encourage him to ask questions that make you both red-faced. His comfort hinges on your receptivity and response. Be proactive and courageous with opening the dialogue about things "weird" but crucial to the life of your boy. It's okay to start slow with a simple analogy or metaphor like Ben's fire and water in the Awaken stage. But move quickly if your son is 10 or older. He likely knows more than you think. Invite your son to ask you questions. Admit your embarrassment. Laugh. Joke. But give it to him head-on. If you don't, those other 'teachers' will.

A few parting thoughts on sex. As you talk with your son, think IV drip, not fire hose. It's not a 'one and done' sort of thing. Save your two-minute drill. Sexuality needs to be a long thread of conversation between a boy and his dad. Now, don't let that statement stress you. You don't need to manufacture times for dialogue. You'll be surprised at opportunities that appear out of nowhere. I've delved into conversations about conception while cooking eggs. We've talked gender when sorting through a jar of old nuts and bolts. We've sat in the sun and pondered why a girl's bike doesn't have a top bar but a boy's does. All of these are gateways to short, simple and useful talks about pieces and parts. Roles and gender. Your son doesn't want, and can't handle the fire hose approach. Don't overwhelm him with a two-minute drill about procreation and positioning. He needs to know the mechanics, absolutely. Sex is a potent and fragile gift. Help your boy traverse the cultural minefield of human sexuality. Be his trusted, available, approachable teacher.

Wrap-up

This Activate stage is the gateway to manhood for your boy. Reality is bringing to bear the first whispers of "Do I have what it takes to be a man?" for your son. As he watches you and interacts with his peers he will hear whisper of unworthiness. He may start to doubt that he will ever grow to be a genuine man. Boys 10-13 years old stand on the doorstep of adolescence. Waiting, wondering, anxious, curious. It's a critical time for dad to be engaged. Intentional.

Lock in on the essential power of imitation because it will someday disappear. Your boy is looking to grown men for examples of manly living. Be the man you want your boy to be. Clearly communicate to him a vision for manhood. Show and tell him how it's done. Activate your boy's inherent manliness through initiation into the community of men. Celebrate him with a memorable ceremony. Welcome him to manhood.

What you do in the Awaken and Activate stages lays the foundation for what's next. Your boy's journey to adulthood doesn't stop. At some point it will be too late to work on what you want him to get from you. Prioritize your time, conversations and experiences and help his boyhood die—because it must.

Manhood Backpack / Activate Stage

Big Idea / Be the man you want your son to be.
Call to Action / Create rites of passage that welcome your son to the starting line of manhood.

Options for Action
01 / Create a Man Wall
02 / Have a night or weekend away for 'the talk'
03 / Go backpacking (bring physical challenge to a Man-cation)
04 / Go on an extended fishing and/or hunting trip
05 / Have a Lord of the Rings movie marathon
06 / Go on mountain bike excursions
07 / Play paintball/air soft together
08 / Take an historical tour together (Underground Railroad experience, Gettysburg, DC)
09 / Encourage your boy to play an instrument
10 / If gifted in the arts, have him try-out for a part in the local theatre or enter artwork in local contests

Stage 03 Transfer

(Ages 13-17)

"Courage is almost a contradiction in terms. It means a strong desire to live taking the form of readiness to die."

– G.K. Chesterton

"My father used to play with my brother and me in the yard. Mother would come out and say, "You're tearing up the grass." "We're not raising grass," my dad would reply, "We're raising boys.""

– Harmon Killebrew

Chris De Man

Deere Strike

Colored in gaudy green and yellow, John Deere is a bulwark of Americana. Rugged. Reliable. Trusted. Even in my dreams, I never owned one. Long ago I resigned myself to a destiny of off-brand mowing drudgery.

Well, I resigned too early. Through a series of fortunate events, I was able to add a Deere to my stable of lawn care equipment. I fondly remember that first season with my Deere. With aplomb I tamed a robust crop of spring dandelions. Summer crabgrass? Child's play. Fall leaves? Mincemeat! I was in lawn mowing ecstasy. It was joyous to manage my little piece of creation with the real deal—Mr. J.D.

You might think my affection for a lawn tractor a bit over-the-top. But if you're a Deere owner, you know of what I speak. It's kind of like Jeep owners who plaster on their car, "It's a Jeep thing." Well, I have a 'Deere thing.' But my 'thing' goes beyond my tractor's turf-taming abilities.

On my desk sits a photo of my John Deere. Don't misunderstand. This is not idolatry (and yes, a picture of my wife is very close by). The photo is not to admire, but to remember. It's a picture of the front grill of my tractor—cracked—shattered, really. Beyond repair. A unique photo, for sure. Why? It makes me a better father. Here's the story.

I knew the day would come. It had to. That day when my Deere affections hit head-on with male pre-pubescent driving aspirations. I was reticent to allow my son behind the wheel of my cherished green and yellow friend. But such hand-offs are a manhood requirement—a rite of passage. Yet not everything required is simple, easy or enjoyable. After some overly-detailed and much-repeated instruction, my good ole' J.D. launched out of the garage with it's rookie driver grinning uncontrollably.

I tried my best to control the experience. You know, setup my son with a confidence building 'first mow.' Lots of straight-away with all landscaping (and family pets) safely out of the mowing path. I paced nervously inside the house. I snuck occasional glances out the window. I listened to the speed of the engine and the hum of the blades. Not too fast; not too slow. Things were progressing nicely. My heart rate had settled and my boy was exuberant in this step toward manhood. I was growing; he was growing. Then, in the midst of this Norman Rockwell moment, it happened.

Balancing Act

Cue the commercial.

I'll finish my story in a bit. I share it to illustrate a necessary and difficult dynamic between a dad and his son. A dynamic of transfer. Transfer of what? Freedom and responsibility—from you, to him.

To help understand this transfer, visualize a simple teeter totter. Now, hang with me. I know talk of teeter-tottering is a bit juvenile, even unmanly at this stage of the manhood journey. But for a moment, dad, picture you and your son on a teeter-totter. You're at the bottom position. The position of power. Control. Meanwhile your son is suspended. Legs dangling. Out of control. He can't move or change his circumstance. In many ways, he's helpless. Completely dependent on you. He has very little freedom or responsibility when it comes to teetering or tottering.

The unbalanced teeter-totter is what the father-son relationship often looks like in the pre-adolescent years. Since birth you've dictated much of what your boy would do, when he would do it and with whom. All of your son's experiences, interactions and decisions were directed, or at least substantially influenced by you. That was good, and right. Your son needs your guidance and protection. But now he's a young man. He seeks ownership, responsibility and freedom—all necessary components of authentic manhood. So things must change. The transfer begins as the teeter-totter moves.

This process of transfer is normal and expected, but none the less difficult. It's a precarious balancing act that must be nurtured, guarded, and in many ways earned by your son. Trust between you and your son is the fulcrum of the teeter-totter. A strong and trusting pivot will make for better balance and a smoother transfer.

Perhaps in your own growing-up you experienced some less than pleasant teeter-tottering. Ever been subjected to the 'I'll keep you at the top and taunt you' scenario? How about 'I'll jump off and let you free-fall to the ground then laugh maniacally' treatment? As dads who love our sons, we must work hard to avoid either extreme. We can't dictate and control our boys indefinitely. We have to let them down. The teeter-totter must move—smoothly and gently. Too much freedom too quickly means free-fall. Too much control yields frustration and perhaps rebellion. Dads must do the careful, intentional work of bringing balance to the teeter-totter of manhood as we shift freedom and responsibility for life to our sons.

When your boy is eighteen, the transfer should be complete. You and your son should sit in a balanced position. Eye-to-eye. Man-to-man. Trusting each other. Your son is fully free, and completely responsible for his life. He is an independent man.

Despite the simplicity of the image, teeter tottering with our sons is precarious and tricky. As a dad, it is a stark and sometimes painful realization that you are not in control. Our boys do grow-up (at least physically). We have been called to shape them with manly character that exudes an attractive and active love for God, and others. Such shaping comes by allowing our sons to take appropriate risks with their freedom. To make their own choices and then follow with responsibility.

Ceremony

So when do you, as dad, start moving the teeter totter in earnest? Movement does happen in very small ways during your son's elementary years. But with the onset of adolescence, the transfer of freedom and responsibility must be an ongoing part of conversation between you and your son.

Unfortunately, adolescence is not punctual. It arrives when it arrives. Some of our sons will be tail-draggers. Others, early adopters. Late bloomer or quick-starter, the age of 13 is a great time for you to formalize the transfer process with your son. Thirteen is typically the gateway for all boys to puberty, peers and pimples. It's the definitive and ominous threshold between boyish things and manly things.

Crossing that threshold deserves unique recognition. An experience. A big-time marker in the journey to manhood that can be commemorated and celebrated. A rite of passage. It may not involve killing a lion, but it does involve the beginning of the end of boyish things. A ceremony provides an Ebenezer—a remembering stone—which you and your son can revisit many times in the years ahead. It provides context for man-to-man discussions about sex, marriage, work and serving others. And, this welcoming ceremony brings clarity to our sons in their becoming men. It provides a definitive event and distinct point in their life when they were welcomed and initiated into the community of men.

Dad, that first seed of manly community is established by you. It starts with your friends, mentors and relatives. Introduce your son to this community. Engage it—together and separately—and draw on its collective wisdom. It should be a life-source for both of you. Don't raise your son alone. It is better to glean from other trusted, godly men. We all have blind spots and inadequacies. Allow the manhood community to bring a fuller development to your son's character through intentional interactions. It will enhance and smooth your teeter-tottering.

Channeling

An area ripe for turmoil during your son's teen years is the expression of his sexuality. Increased attraction and interaction with young women through conversations, social media, texting, phone calls and possibly dating means there is much new ground to tread—for both of you. Girls are coming at him like a Gatling Gun. Traversing the teen years can feel like walking over coals. Each step needs careful placement as the fires of sexuality rage for your boy.

By this point, you and your son should have had 'the talk.' In fact, you should have had many talks. But now is not the time to congratulate yourself. The birds and bees may have flown, but the mission isn't over. More than ever, young men need consistent, pointed, and clear instruction regarding male sexuality and appropriate ways to interact with young women.

Perhaps you remember the sexual tension of your teen years?

For me, high school was a non-stop dating game. Girls teased. Guys gazed. There was coupling and uncoupling. Hallway gossip perpetuated the cycle of 'going together' and the infamous 'break-up.' Back seat romps and mythic exploits colored locker room talk.

But the dating game has changed. Today, desires of all sorts are fanned into flame. Outlets for sexual expression are offered eagerly and unreservedly. The thirst for pleasure trumps restraint. The lust for new and different is insatiable. Such a culture is quick-sand for a teenage boy.

Your boy will be pulled toward women—real, imagined or virtual. Childhood friends who were 'just girls' become objects of extended stares and potential 'girl friends.' He'll pursue, and be pursued—aggressively. In his book *iParent* Don Pearson suggests, "Young girls shock boys through sensual words and images, arranging and leading them about like dogs on a leash." (p.68) The boiling hormones of a teenage boy matched with a young woman too eager to hand-over her body yields exceptional volatility. Your son needs you, and other good men to guide him through this jungle of temptation. Your son needs your strong and consistent protection. He needs boundaries. The battle for purity reaches a fevered pitch as he sprints toward manhood.

But let's be clear. This isn't about behavior management. You can't just hope and pray your boy keeps his pants on and hands off. What's churning inside your son are elements that will fortify him to love in ways that are sacrificial and manly. Sexual tension is an unavoidable component of manhood. It is God-given drive intended to provide for, and protect women and children. Harnessing and shaping this power surge of masculinity requires persistence and discipline.

So help your son train his will. Talk straight with him about preserving his heart—and his body. Work together to establish guidelines and parameters that aid his discernment with relationships. Open a dialogue about what's desirable in a woman. A place to start might be telling him what you admire about your spouse. If you're a single dad, talk to your son about his mother and what attracted you to her. Perhaps you're presently pursuing a woman. Show your son how to honor, respect and care for her. Then bridge to talking about specific girls your son shows affection for. Be involved in his interests.

Your boy might be slow in the pursuit of young women. Your patience might get stretched. But in the waiting, don't stop talking. Keep the dialogue alive with conversation about healthy, honorable relationships with women before emotions cloud clear thinking or situations develop that rock you both on your heels. And all the while, keep challenging him with physical, mental and emotional discipline. With purity. Point him toward a sold-out, life time covenant with one woman. Keep in front of him the admonition, "He who finds a wife finds what is good and receives favor from the Lord." (Proverbs 18:22) Foster his excitement for commitment and responsibility. Grow in him a desire to protect and provide for a future wife and family.

One way to grow that desire and leverage the energy of a teenage boy is through work. A real man needs to provide for himself and others. So as your son moves toward adulthood, channel his energy into developing a solid work ethic. Start by giving him opportunities to work and earn at home. Be creative. Transition some of your household load to him. As you do, he'll walk taller and listen better. Show him how to save, give and spend. Talk about expectations for his earning. Make him responsible for specific expenses—and stick to it. It's good training that develops responsibility and gives your son a taste of what it's like to meet the demands of daily living.

I Die. He Lives.

Now, the conclusion to my Deere story.

The engine slowed. The blades disengaged. The mower stopped. I found a window and cast a bug-eyed stare. My view was partially obstructed, but I could see my son circling the mower. My mind played a dozen scenarios in a matter of seconds. I sarcastically mumbled to my wife, "This isn't going to be good." After several minutes of circling, kneeling, pausing and doing nothing my son was back at the helm. The engine throttled to full speed and mowing continued.

My curiosity red-lined. A twitch of anger raced down my temple. Worst-case scenarios played on the screen of my mind. The circumstance was ripe for a potent father/son interaction. An interaction heavy with growing-up, letting-go and man-making. As the noise of the tractor echoed in the garage, and then subsided, I sighed. And waited. And prayed. Then the door opened.

The rest of the story I'll leave to your wondering. The truth is captured in that photo on my desk. When I look at that picture, it's like picking a scab. The pain is renewed. Selfish pain born in materialism. Vicarious pain for my son and his mistake. Soul pain because of life's brokenness.

That pain pushes me deeper into my fathering. It broadens my view and helps me see that life is bigger than me—and my tractor. To see that I'm not in control. To see that bringing life to my son's manhood means some things in me must die.

G.K. Chesterton said, "A true soldier fights not because he hates what is in front of him, but because he loves what is behind him." Loving what's behind means I do the hard work of true manly living. It means I accept being broken and the moments of clarity and self-reflection brokenness brings. It means I expand gratitude for my heavenly Father who watches me break the metaphorical tractor grill day after day—yet responds with grace.

Wrap-up

Adolescence can be a fearful time—for you, and your son. Letting him down from the top of the teeter-totter is a frightening proposition. As dads, we have to let go of control and give our sons the freedom to make mistakes, accept responsibility for important things and gracefully guide them into manhood. It's a process of dying. Your son is putting to death his boyhood. You are killing desires you hold too closely. Making a man from a boy is one of the most courageous things you will do. Draw strength from God and His Word, and be constantly in prayer as you walk the manhood path with your boy.

At times that means failure. We will fail. Our sons will fail. The teeter-totter might jar with a bump. Or, maybe we sit too long at the bottom causing frustration for our boys. Balancing freedom and responsibility will push you and your son to the edge. At times you'll be frustrated and discouraged. Neither of you will know what to do. You'll see-saw on the teeter-totter.

Such is the pot-holed path to manhood. It's okay. Live in the tension, and keep talking. Cast and re-cast your vision for manhood. Have plenty of man-to-man talks like were mentioned in the Activate stage. Stay firmly fastened to the goal of complete transfer of freedom and responsibility to your boy. Stay focused on the vision of your son living as a biblically authentic man. A man, characterized by responsible, loving, selfless, courageous servant-leadership. A man looking for reward from God, not the pleasures of this world.

Manhood Backpack / Transfer Stage

Big Idea / A man must die for a boy to live.
Call to Action / Transfer freedom and responsibility from you to your son.

Options for Action

01 / Take a quad or motorcycle trip together

02 / Have him handle the lawn-mowing and other 'manly' household chores

03 / Encourage him to get a part-time job

04 / Send him on a big city tour—perhaps alone?

05 / Hunting experience together

06 / Attend an auto show in a big city like Detroit, Chicago or LA

07 / Have him manage a bank account for yearly purchases and needs (clothing, entertainment)

08 / If inclined toward reading and writing, let him start a blog or encourage submitting written works for publishing

09 / Setup regular opportunities for him to volunteer in the community

Stage 04 Release

(Ages 18+)

"Far better it is to dare mighty things, to win glorious triumphs, even though checkered by failure, than to take rank with those poor spirits who neither enjoy nor suffer too much, because they live in the gray twilight that knows not victory nor defeat."

– Teddy Roosevelt

"Adversity toughens manhood, and the characteristic of the good or the great man is not that he has been exempt from the evils of life, but that he has surmounted them."

– Patrick Henry

Don Pearson
Risk

The fact that everyone laughed had nothing to do with the speaker being funny. He wasn't. They needed an outlet; he provided one.

Most of the parents sitting in the auditorium were fresh off multiple trips. They'd been dragging precious cargo into dorm rooms, setting up lofts and attempting to kill their feelings with small projects. Wireless Internet hooked-up. Drawers filled. Toiletries stacked in the shared bathroom.

This next stage of life, where our sons join the military, head to university or opt for closer-to-home alternatives mixes hope and fear like a blender. Rites of passage mess with dad as much as they do son and if not, we've come to a disjointed release or a fabricated launch. Why? Because risk is unavoidable on the path to manhood. It can't be negotiated downward towards the safety zone. Can't be detoured. Can't be tamed.

The stages our sons pass through are like narrows where the water bunches and gets ramrodded through. Where boulders and logjams change a translucent river into a cauldron of white water.

It's time for the great release. Our son is moving on. Or should be.

Some of us are ready. Our sons are in a pretty good place. Others hope that whatever happens at the next stage can help fill-in some of the holes. Still others remain hesitant, juggling anxiety about economic uncertainties or delayed maturity. Maybe you're just perplexed that America seems to be producing more video games than men?

What is the essence of the risk between the fourth and fifth stages of manhood? As we jam his car full or trek to the dorm with another load, what is really happening? For you, and for him?

Going Alone

Your son must find his own way; chart his own path. And it's the vulnerability of this situation that must be faced and preserved. On the next section of river, he canoes alone. His development depends on it. Whether your tendency is to retain your parental claws (studying the geography of college choices so that he's not too far away) or wave off his choices with a detached frustration, the essence remains. He must go it alone.

Will he do his laundry? Was he taught how to do laundry? Do you leave him rolls of quarters for the machine? Could he identify a washing machine if it was inserted in a lineup of appliances?

Whether the light-duty issues of a laundry quandary and car maintenance, or the heavy-duty realties of homosexual opportunists and imprisoning debt, he walks alone. At least he begins alone. Forms of accountability and community may come—come from his development, not ours.

It's precisely this aloneness that culture has attempted to eradicate. One of the most alarming disconnects from historical wisdom occurs in the way the West has abolished male initiation rites.

In almost all cultures men are not born, they are made. Much more than for women, cultures have traditionally demanded initiation rites specifically for the boys. It is almost as if the biological experiences of menstruation and childbirth are enough wisdom lessons for women, but invariably men must be tried, limited, challenged, punished, hazed, circumcised, isolated, starved, stripped, and goaded into maturity. The pattern is nearly universal, and the only real exceptions are the recent secular West (Richard Rohr, From Wild Man to Wise Man, p.31)

A friend of mine contends that it's precisely our unwillingness to remove our parental hands that has led to extended adolescence. In a culture where most college graduates will move back home, he took an aggressive, anti-cultural stance with his kids. Choosing high school graduation as the release date, he cut all ties. Financial. Room and board. Cell phone. Automobile. And he did it well. With a decade of training in financial responsibility and the inevitable school of hard knocks, his two kids walked away never to return to his house of entitlements. You might argue that if he'd had three kids, the story may have changed. And you may be right. But the fact remains, his move stands out as rare.

Dual Risk

By now, you know that bringing a boy to manhood has as much to do with you as it does your son. Rites of passage bring both father and son to the precipice. How authentic are you in your walk with the Lord? How do you face your own uncertainties? There is the correlation: (1) How do you enter your problems, (2) How will you allow him to face his?

At some point your son must be confronted with the following reality: I don't know what to do, but I know that if I don't do something, I'm dead. And he must face this often and alone. It forges the authentic man. The boy sheds the well-oiled skin of parents who greased his path, who made life workable for him.

The real father identifies those things that formerly protected his child and now labels them as enemies- enemies of his growth, preventers of his emerging manhood. Is it you as a father? Is it his mother? Is it his community? His culture? You've seen the athletic leagues, right? The ones the parents set up for their kids to succeed? Adults travel to great lengths, spending thousands of dollars and wearing out automobiles. If the regular sporting options weren't working, no problem. Find a new coach, a new team. Make a new tier. Call it the 'travel team' or the 'elite team.' Guarantee that your kid succeeds.

Abandonment

A strange irony exists in all rites of passage. Remember the rungu story in the Awaken stage? A well-planned time of abandonment is truly empowering, while overprotection is merely prolonged abandonment. We abandon our boys when we extend the umbrella of provision and protection.

Earlier this year I had the extraordinary privilege of touring the Western mountains and canyons with my son.

On motorcycles.

Zion, Bryce, Grand Canyon, Route 66, Death Valley.

You'll note that I said motorcycles, not motorcycle. The slight difference in words (plural instead of singular) nearly caused me cardiac arrest. Each night when I laid my head on the pillow in a new campground or motel room, the foreboding came. Replays of the day. Uncertainties about tomorrow.

Which route to choose? Around the mountain or over it? Who goes first? Do we skirt the heavy traffic of Vegas or plow through it, going neck and neck with 18-wheelers? You see, prior to the trip my son had very little experience on a bike. And here's the catch. How does one gain experience? It's almost as if the hyper-parental camp says 'remove all risk' because with risk comes potential regret. Remove rites of passage. But what's the hidden message in that approach?

Can a boy become a man without risk?

Can a man father without the very real potential for regret?

Can the boy gain experience without…experience?

On one occasion during our motorcycle adventure we had 40 knot crosswinds for six hours. Those winds turned the desert into a giant dust bowl. I had very little time or ability to glance ahead to my boy's bike as I struggled just to keep mine on the road. We both maneuvered through the treacherous conditions. You can imagine how dinner that night took on a different note than the meal just 24-hours earlier. Shared risk. Survival. Lessons learned and stories told. The stuff of ancient lore.

You are passing through these stages correctly when the journey messes with the father as much as it does his son. It takes risk to put a four-year-old on a baby quad, risk to put a twelve-year-old on a John Deere and risk to watch your son traverse 2,000 miles of canyons, deserts and mountains on a Honda Shadow.

Taking Inventory

As you interact with your son prior to his launch, take inventory of risks on both sides of the equation. His and yours. What is this costing you? How much lip-biting are you doing? And what deliberate risks are you planning to take?

How about him? How connected to reality is he as you assess his plans? When it comes to risk-taking, would you say he's overdoing it or underachieving?

David was concerned about his son. His 19-year old son. He'd graduated the year before—a year in which he'd been in the middle of a very successful football program. It dominated his life. Yet the following year he seemed aimless and apathetic. So the father talked with me and wondered if I had an idea about a program that would fit his son's needs.

A proper inventory of this situation would include several, painful assessments. Cross examination. The initial determination reflects on the father's role going forward. His involvement, at whatever level, is crucial to evaluate. The next issue centers on what is best for his son. Floundering is not all bad—especially, if it is allowed to happen so that manhood can emerge. In this sense, the kid's development may be delayed if another 'top down' program comes his way.

Experiential Learning

Experience is a great teacher. When our sons are younger, we often create experiences for that very reason. We want them to learn. As they grow up, we have a broader menu to choose from as more experiences become available. Not only does the menu get larger, the opportunities are more frequent. That's why you'll often hear parents talk about life speeding up. Time seems to be measured by events rather than a math formula.

Stage four experiences might include:

01 / Job

02 / College

03 / Military

04 / Vocational school

05 / Apprenticeship

06 / Mission trips

07 / Study abroad

08 / Road trips

09 / New relationships

10 / New influencers

Your job is simply to keep the discussion alive. Since your son will pass through a large number of experiences, the opportunity to process life becomes almost non-stop.

When my son first told me about his spring break plans, one critical thought after another pounded through my head. Holding them back (refusing to react verbally) created the need for a second Hoover Dam. But what do you expect? He was 20 at the time, and I was near 50.

His plans involved him and four buddies leaving Lee University in Tennessee and doing the loop tour of California. Head out the southern route, go north along the coast of California and return east through Montana and the Dakotas. As you track our conversation (below) see if you can determine who is speaking.

"Whose car you taking?"

Silence. "Probably mine"

"How many are going?"

"Five or six, depending on if John can get out of work."

"How long do you have?"

"A week."

"How are you paying for gas?"

We haven't talked about that yet but probably whoever is driving.

"Do they all drive a stick?"

"Kelvin does…not sure about the other guys."

At this point the conversation can go several ways. From a 50 year old's perspective there isn't one thing about the plan that seems workable. From a 20 year old's perspective….wait a minute, there is no perspective. There's been no experience.

Which of the following responses would you choose at this point?

A / Well son, the plan is not workable. I recommend staying on campus and working so that you can have something to apply towards your final tuition bill

B / That trip reminds me of something that my buddies and I tried to pull off at about the same stage of life

C / That's about the dumbest thing I've ever heard

D / Sounds interesting. I'll enjoy following your plans as they develop

E / Other than you won't fit in the car, can't afford it and don't have enough time, I think you're on to something

My son's ability to dream and create his own experiences is precisely what is so crucial at this stage. Keep the conversation alive and hold off on your perspective unless specifically asked for. The realities of life will solve themselves. Who pays? Who drives? Will we fit? Do we have enough time? That's the small stuff. The wonder, the dream, the scheming, the sketching out a route on a map. This is stuff where legends are born, where lessons are learned. Where men are made.

When your son was young, you did the planning. The dreaming. You worked on the details of the man-cation (with a bit of help from your boy). But at this Release stage, the last thing you should do is plan and control. Instead, let your son take control of the natural experiences he encounters. Let him plan-out his dreams and be ready if he needs a sounding board. Plenty of dark things are coming his way, many that will provide a different kind of experience base from which to work.

Arousal Addiction

Today's young man must navigate what psychologist Phillip Zimbardo calls 'arousal addiction.' The surrounding culture and its virtual saturation creates an environment where young boys get digitally rewired. Zimbardo references two main ways this occurs: video games and pornography. Admittedly, we've heard enough about these concerns to cause our eyes to glaze over. But here's the new issue. If the addiction is for what's new and different, novel and fresh, then boys are "totally out of sync in traditional classes, which are analog, static, interactively passive. They're also out of sync in romantic relationships, which build gradually and subtly." (http://www.ted.com/talks/

zimchallenge.html)

And your son is not alone. Notice the challenge in your own life. The sexually aggressive girl—whether during a commercial in a football game or through internet pop-ups—has redefined women. Her new sexuality is suddenly nothing more than man-like. She wants it now. She wants more. She's always ready. Such a lie mocks your relationship with your wife. Doing porn and making love should be a universe apart, yet culture seeks to define them as one in the same.

Talking about sex with your son in this stage becomes eerily similar. You're both men. You both live in the same culture. You both face the same lies.

Manhood Backpack / Release Stage

Big Idea / Release your young man into independent, authentic manly living.

Call to Action / Stop covering for your boy and greasing the skids.

Options for Action

01 / College
02 / Full Time Job
03 / Military
04 / Mission trip
05 / Apprenticeship
06 / Road trip
07 / Study abroad
08 / Peace Corp

Stage 05 Return

Living As A Real Man

"There's a lot of blood, sweat and guts between dreams and success."

– Paul "Bear" Bryant

"No man has ever risen to the stature of spiritual manhood until he has found that it is finer to serve somebody else than it is to serve himself."

– Woodrow Wilson

Don Pearson

Now what?

Mark stared out the window as the miles disappeared behind him. As his wife dozed, he thought back four years to when they'd dropped Clay off at college. A shiver escaped and he refocused on the road. This day would be different. Clay was coming home.

The interstate—somewhat familiar due to two trips per college year—continued to unwind, as did his emotions. To think that Clay was graduating already.

Mark shook his head in disbelief. Time was speeding up and unlike his car, he couldn't restrain it with cruise control. He blinked, attempting to wash away the next thought, but he lingered too long. All that tuition. All that investment. For what purpose?

His son, like the vast majority of college graduates, was moving back home. His plan was to scour the universe for a job, notwithstanding the fact that they don't make jobs to match the debt hole he'd dug. He dated some in college. But like half of his friends seemed immobilized in that area of life.

Mark let his mind drift aimlessly, wondering how this new stage would unfold, how his son would gain the confidence necessary to stare-down the down economy. In fact, the more he reflected, the more he wondered how he would have faced the world his son was stepping into.

Each of us maintains a watch list about this stage of life.

A list of three items: Career. Marriage. Kids.

These are the mile markers that have typically defined a young man's final transition to adulthood. And regardless of the strides your son makes towards these, the challenge lies in the surrounding culture. If he lands a career early, he must still maneuver among friends who largely don't live that way. If he beats the odds and gets married before 25, a host of 'out of favor' parasites eat away at that marriage. Parasites like a culture of purposeful drinking, social pressure to enjoy the benefits of relationships without commitment, and an economic worldview that elevates earnings above being married with children. The intimidating reality for us dads is that our sons will not have these three items (career, marriage, family) secured by age 30. In 1960, 70% of men had these in the bag by their 30th birthday. Today, that figure hovers near 26%.

I recently had a conversation with a trusted friend. We both have a couple of unmarried kids in their mid-20's and we were discussing strategy and attempting to steal ideas from each other. In what ways had we contributed to their extended adolescence? In light of current culture, what issues are we facing that our parents never had to deal with? What adjustments must be made?

Consider this: none of these four are slackers. All remain committed to pursuing a calling and their work ethics are beyond good. One is doing graduate level study, one has a beginning teaching job, the third is pursuing a calling where financial reward is often deferred while the fourth is doing mission work.

Some questions that my friend and I wrestle with:

Cell phone bills / Who pays? Is there a scenario where a shared payment works?

Car insurance / When does this finally transfer from father to son? At 16? 18? College graduation?

Loaner car / What happens when their piece of junk is in for repair again? What do they drive to get to their demanding, underpaying job?

That job market for 16-29 year olds is at its worst level since World War II. Period. And the issue of whether or not your son moves ahead of the pack doesn't change his overall culture. His space is dominated by harsh realities. His friends, their attitudes, their choices.

The cultural shift from the time we left high school to the present realities our sons face has two profound elements that will affect how we parent in this last stage:

Exponential / Speed is speeding up with the net result that cultural change happens more often and is more seismic. Technology delivers change at lightning speed, guaranteeing that the only thing under your son's feet is a constantly shifting foundation.

Gender / Healthy gender, in both boys and girls, has come under such attack that distortion is commonplace. The rules by which boys and girls have historically 'played house' are now rewritten.

Being the right type of dad during this last stage of the manhood journey is multi-faceted.

The Process is the Product

We can no longer hold out our traditional checklist as if it's the final product. Because of current unique cultural dynamics, get a real job and get married cannot be the primary focus. If you find your conversations continually gravitating towards these metrics, you'll likely find a one-sided lecture. And you're the speaker.

The collision of many social factors may call you to a different game plan. As parents we must shift our focus from the product to the process that our sons are working through. Character building now becomes number one. It's what we pray about, re-examine in our own lives and it also becomes the focus of talks with our sons. Fathers used to have the luxury of knowing that marriage and career would do its own work on boys. Once the boy crossed those off his list, life would inherently provide the process by which he grew up. There was no choice to the matter.

Scott met me for coffee and after a round of small talk, he paused and glanced out the window. He started talking, hesitated, rephrased in his mind, and finally said, "I just don't know what to tell him. He's got a job. Kind of. But there's no way it's going to allow him to get anywhere. He wants to pursue writing and perhaps another degree. But that'd take decades to translate into anything, even if he turned out to be good at it."

Scott faces a common dilemma. His son accomplished everything a young man was expected to. Good grades in high school followed by a business degree from college. Now he was piecing together part time work until something better came along. Yet notice the kinds of things Scott and I talked about: jobs, careers, grades, degrees. They're all types of measurements, right? Culturally agreed upon milestones that should have come with a guaranteed result. But they didn't. And most indicators point to a very different type of future for Scott's son—and possibly yours.

This shift from the traditional becomes the unique privilege of today's fathers. They enter the same risk they're hopeful their sons will embrace: I don't know what to do but I better do something. What is that something?

A shift away from cultural milestones can become a shift to character building. Consider these subtle changes in conversation:

From career to work ethic.

From marriage to movement.

These quiet shifts suddenly allow our sons to focus on things within their control. The prevailing winds of multiple part-time jobs become the playground where they learn the power of a strong work ethic. In addition, our sons invest energy into their dreams and passions. Your son will use his part-time employment to fund where he wants to go. Sure, he probably can't go as fast or bring a wife along yet. Or maybe, without a wife he can move more quickly. But movement is the key.

Pretend that Lance is subbing an average of three times a week as he looks for a full time teaching position. What core dream does he have into which he can pour himself during the other days? What kinds of risks unfold? Is he stepping into them with regular guts? And as he does so, what conversations can take place regarding work ethic?

The process begins to become the product. Whether embracing and entering fear or gaining traction in a relationship, he faces the same essential challenges of a boy from fifty years ago who just happened to wake up and find himself married and starting a career.

Dreaming

Ironically, the emerging man begins to clarify what he was born for. *Wait a minute*, thinks the discerning father. *Wasn't that what college was for?* Good question. Yet an increasing number of guys are delving deeper into their core calling after college. Dreams now begin to align more closely with his gift mix.

How can a father enter this? First, let's be honest. Very few kids know themselves well enough at 17 years of age to stake the next six decades of their life on. It's often the worldview education that they receive in college or the military, as opposed to the career education, that sparks this deeper journey.

Eric shook his head and simply said, "Forty-seven thousand dollars."

The topic of college debt was on the table, temporarily interrupted as hot-n-sour soup splashed down in front of us.

"I can't believe it," he said. "It's so clear now. I have no idea why I stayed with psychology."

With great passion, Eric took me through his change of perspective. From a BA in Psychology and it's somewhat fuzzy promise of what a job could look like, to a plan for the next four years of his life and the very specific field of mission work in Haiti.

As the meal came to an end, I picked up the tab. He was, after all, $47k in the hole.

Fathering at this stage looks much like it does when a friend asks you advice about a career change. Notice the absence of anxiety? Sure, you feel for the guy, but you're able to rise above it and give an objective opinion. What he's good at, and not so good at.

Shoulder to Shoulder

What your son needs most is inspiration. This comes from the shoulder-to-shoulder probing where he excels. Perhaps what he was born for. Deep practice, working in the area of his passions, will flow as you encourage and inspire him. Just remember this old proverb: advice not asked for is a form of rejection. Let it come when it comes. No need to force it.

Some men end their formal careers after thirty years only to go into what 'they've always wanted to do.' Others have several false starts at the beginning yet find their sweet spot earlier.

Fathering during this stage is about friendship and occasional advice whereas 'parenting' is virtually eliminated. Although we'll always have that parental thing hanging around, our own risk involves burying it. Rather than focusing on direct, face-to-face questions, consider discussing things from a shoulder-to-shoulder vantage point (leaning on a railing, looking out across a field).

The joy of this stage is that the parenting responsibility is finished and a sense of 'normal' returns. Anxiety will always exist because we live in a very broken world. But the way our relationship unfolds is radically different than when you had the God-given responsibility to parent.

His World

The three biggies exist for your son as they did for you and your father. Sex, money and power are older than dirt. And what do we say about them? They are the playgrounds where we come to know God. They are where the frustrations of life beat us down yet attach a gift on the back end. It's not about us after all. As C.S. Lewis said, "it takes two worlds to make sense of one."

God is interested in us living the larger story where His character and plan occupy our attentions and our affections.

Five men in their 80's gathered for their once-a-week breakfast at a local restaurant. And as they liked to say, the number of seats needed each week was never a guarantee. My own accountability friendship happened during that same hour and place. And on occasion, my friend and I listened in as these guys bantered life back and forth.

One time, the topic surfaced as to whether life was really changing or whether the problems kids faced were really no different than what they had to deal with. What caught my attention was the passion with which they debated. Nearly evenly split, they wrangled about sex issues for quite some time. You can be the judge about the deep realities of the male struggle, but few of us can argue the exponential rate of change in our son's world.

Sex

The feminist movement was the greatest influence of the 20th century. Most agree. Traditionally a girl used the power of her body to convert a man's lust to love within the confines of a committed, marital relationship. Now she trades it as a commodity, dispensing it with apparently less thought than what she wants for lunch.

Sex is free.

Separated from its created partner of procreation, pleasure becomes the dominant, singular value. Though the girl often uses sex in the attempt to jump-start a relationship, she overestimates that the man will tag along and forge a domestic commitment. This girl is aggressive and it's her very alpha stance that sets the man back on his heels, enabling him to remain a boy. He stalls. He drifts further from the ability to commit than when she first encountered him.

The argument as to whose fault it is, male or female, becomes circular. A perpetual motion machine that is steadily fueled by culture. He avoids responsibility. She arranges and controls. Whether the virtual world of porn, the titillating world of sexting or the very real world of hooking up, sex trends tell the child-man that orgasms are free.

This is the world where your son will forge his manhood. The sophisticated sexual artillery that he must face makes ours look like single-shot BB guns.

Money

The economy sucks. And our sons have no practical way to compare it to history. Corporate greed, debt to GDP ratios, Ponzi schemes at the government level and big banking seem to be the order of the day. Lots of fleas. No dogs.

His prospects of landing a suitable career—one that allows him to pursue and provide for a family—remains the worst since World War II. This, his second playground, provides ample frustration to drive him to God. The exact spot you want him.

I had an interesting talk with a guy the other day. We're both in our early fifties. We were marveling at the change in our own perspective in terms of retirement. We entered our forties with plenty of money fear, anxiety over how we'd attain the lofty numbers required to retire. A decade later, we now consider the present economy a gift. Sure it's hard. And yes, it comes with plenty of worry. But the American Dream of retirement was no friend to the mature man of God. Rather, it resembled a thinly veiled return to adolescence. A failed social experiment.

Our sons will need to learn their own lessons that are powerful illustrators against the personal greed and affluence of a materialistic culture where the lies of money are so embedded we all fell asleep on them.

Power

Ironically, the aggressive girl that our sons need to deal with in the sexual realm may also be the girl they compete against in the marketplace. And in this regard, he's losing. For every 100 college degrees that men obtain, women receive 164. And the numbers are equally stunning when we examine the workplace. Manufacturing (long considered manly jobs) is giving ground to careers where social intelligence is valued. Women have now gained over 50% of all managerial jobs. That said, it is no small fact that women also complain about the 'end of men', about the lack of being pursued by them.

The technical issues that our sons will have to work through on this third playground include such challenges as:

Careers vs. Careerism It's the ordering of priorities that has caused marriage and childbearing to fall out of favor. And when it comes to the issue of careerism with women, it's greatly magnified.

Healthy Gender Culture is blurring gender into one. On the sexual front, women are portrayed as men (always ready and always wanting more). In the general area of leadership, everything is up for grabs as we've made it an issue of equality rather than of roles.

Culture of Revenge As disturbing as it may sound, the love-hate relationship between men and women seems exacerbated by a culture that harbors collective anger. While women caustically write articles about the disappearance of men, the child-man fantasizes through revenge porn. A clear loss on either side.

How different is the way of Christ. "For even the son of man did not come to be served, but to serve, and to give his life as a ransom for many." (The Bible | Mark 10:45)

Experience

As you relate with your son through this fifth stage, notice that experiences outpace the time you have to process them. It's like picking cherry tomatoes after a particularly awesome growing season. There are clusters of opportunities from which to talk about real-life manhood.

Sex, money and power tripped up the wisest man to have ever lived, King Solomon. And they'll attempt to wreak havoc on us as well. What becomes increasingly amazing, often to the shock of the father, is that you're on the same plane with your son. He has been integrated into the community of men. From the beginning of this Return stage till the day we die, men face the same harsh realities. Temptations shift playgrounds, women begin announcing football games, money escapes clenched fists, wives speak a foreign language and God uses all of it for our good—even delegating the job of raising sons who return your investment and raise their own sons. Sons who will one day become men that are man-made.

Manhood Backpack / Return Stage

Big Idea / Engage life's complexities and challenges as men working shoulder-to-shoulder.

Call to Action / Let the process be the product of your ongoing, man-to-man relationship.

Options for Action
01 / Road trip together
02 / Hobby sharing
03 / Movie debriefing
04 / Book sharing
05 / Shared business venture
06 / Collaborating ideas
07 / Volunteer together
08 / Establish a tradition together

Time-out

"God knows our situation; He will not judge us as if we had no difficulties to overcome. What matters is the sincerity and perseverance of our will to overcome them."

– C.S. Lewis

"I am an optimist. It does not seem too much use being anything else."

– Winston Churchill

Failure?

A growing number of adult sons are still living with their parents. Some returned after being away, whether at college or a brief try at independence. Others never left.

Multiple factors have caused an increase in this phenomenon. Certain factors are unavoidable, such as a desperate economy. But other issues tend to be more complex such as the increase in helicopter (rescue) parenting or the lack of male rites of passage (a coddling culture which hinders a boy's growth).

If you find yourself in this situation, you'll likely have plenty of company. The important distinction to make concerns the attitude and motivation of your son. For those who are drifting and aimless, belligerent or unteachable, we recommend a good book by Dr. John Townsend, *Boundaries with Teens*. The challenges associated with having a son get a job, become productive, gain confidence or move out of the home can often be traced back to good communication, clear expectations, consequences and follow through.

Regrets?

There may be other dads reading this who live with regrets. Men who, for one reason or another didn't attempt many of the concepts we've discussed. Where do you start, or is it too late?

I've been on plenty of trips with dads and sons where this has been the case. And the interesting deal is that with few exceptions both son and father want it to be different. Sure, they might not admit it (at least not aloud). And in most cases there's plenty of baggage and lots of calluses. But beneath the pain, the longing remains alive.

If this describes your journey in anyway, I recommend doing a trip together with a larger group. Allow the buffer of others to help you begin building memories together. Almost without exception, I find that during a weekend or while on an extended trip, there is a coming together. It might be brief, like an unprotected laugh together. Or a dangerous, unexpected moment when both of you get lost in the larger calling to survive. Or maybe it's a great meal after some extreme physical exertion.

Begin by building shared memories. Eventually you'll find your way back to each other.